Holidays Around the World

Celebrate
Cinco de Mayo

Carolyn Otto
Consultant, Dr. José M. Alamillo

NATIONAL GEOGRAPHIC
WASHINGTON, D.C.

Alain Villa waits to perform with other dancers in Los Angeles, California.

fiestas

Every year, in Mexico and in the United States, we celebrate Cinco de Mayo with fiestas, music, and dance.

music

Cinco de Mayo means the 5th of May in Spanish. The day marks the 1862 victory of the Mexican army over much stronger French forces in the Battle of Puebla. In the U.S., it has become a joyous celebration of Mexican culture.

dance

< A straw sombrero

3

We celebrate our history.

Cinco de Mayo is sometimes confused with Mexico's Independence Day. Mexico had declared its independence from Spain on the 16th of September in 1821. But the newly independent country had problems. Mexico owed money to many other nations, countries that wanted to take advantage of Mexico's land and resources. Mexico even had to fight a war against the United States and lost almost half of its territory.

It was a hard time in Mexico's history. The president of Mexico asked for more time to repay the money and rebuild his country. Everyone agreed, except France.

A historic plaza in downtown Mexico City shows its Spanish roots.

France sent troops across the Atlantic Ocean to Mexico. French soldiers then marched across the country. They met the Mexican army at Puebla, Mexico, near Mexico City, the capital.

v *In 19th-century French costumes, men reenact the Battle of Puebla in San Diego, California.*

We are proud

# of our victory.

∧ Mexicans fight back in the re-created battle. Today, they shoot only powder, not bullets. No one gets hurt.

The French had more soldiers than the Mexicans, and they had better weapons and fancy uniforms. But the Mexican army fought hard. In the end, the Mexicans defeated the French.

Every year, in Puebla and elsewhere, we re-create the famous battle. Some of us pretend to be French troops, and some of us pretend to be the Mexican soldiers. We march in parades to show how the armies marched long ago.

In the United States, we have parades, too. We celebrate our culture with lots of music and dancing.

We celebrate with music and dance.

< *Folk dancers celebrate Cinco de Mayo in Phoenix, Arizona.*

> *Two members of a Mexican-American dance company smile at each other as they perform at the state capitol in Sacramento, California.*

Boys wear cowboy hats or sombreros, and girls wear dresses with ruffled skirts. Mothers braid their girls' hair with ribbons—red, white, and green—the colors of the Mexican flag.

v Marchers in West Saint Paul, Minnesota, proudly display the red, white, and green Mexican flag.

red

< At a Cinco de Mayo celebration in Los Angeles, a girl with ribbons braided into her hair performs with the Ballet Folklorico.

green

white

> A boy in Port Huron, Michigan, sports a traditional Mexican sombrero and a modern jersey displaying Mexico's colors.

11

We have parades.

∧ Members of a lowrider bicycle club join the parade in New York City.

< Dancers of the Americas float glides past the state capitol building in Denver, Colorado.

We ride on floats covered with tissue-paper flowers. In the United States, we entertain the crowd with special cars called lowriders. Some of us ride special lowrider bicycles.

Mariachi bands may march with us, or they might stop to play songs for the people lining the streets. We sometimes perform traditional dances in our colorful costumes.

Musicians from Alma del Sol (Soul of the Sun) play mariachi music during a Cinco de Mayo festival in Scottsdale, Arizona.

∧ *Maracas*

There are so many kinds of music from Mexico! Traditional *ranchera, banda,* mariachi—too many to name. We also have American pop music, hip-hop, and classic rock and roll. In the United States, it is easy to tune our radios to our favorites. Sometimes we make our own music too!

We make our own music.

Our parades lead us

to gatherings in city parks, auditoriums, and playgrounds. Some places hold big festivals. We have crafts and games and learn about Mexican traditions. We have exciting things to see—everything from folklorico dancers to chihuahua fashion shows and races.

∧ *Mejerle the Chihuahua shows off his team spirit in Chandler, Arizona.*

> *A young boy in Denver carries on Mexican traditions by learning how to hold a lasso.*

Los Angeles welcomes hundreds of thousands of people to its 36-block-long celebration, said to be the largest Cinco de Mayo festival in the world.

We have fun!

We hit the piñata!

One of our favorite games is to hit the piñata. A piñata can come in many shapes. It is hollow, so that it can be filled with treats. A blindfolded boy or girl is given a stick or a bat to hit the piñata. Most often they miss. But then someone will finally break the piñata, and candy flies everywhere.

< A donkey piñata

< Cameron Heape decorates the piñata he's making in Independence, Kansas.

> In Syracuse, New York, Kelly O'Sullivan takes her best shot at the piñata.

19

And we eat! At the festivals, we buy tacos, burritos, fried churros, and lemonade—all sorts of good food. But for many of us, the real feast will come later.

In the evenings, we go home with our families. Our fathers and mothers have strung white lights in our back-yards. We get together with our grandparents, our aunts and uncles, and our cousins.

Picnic tables are loaded with food. We eat Mexican food—beans and rice and chicken in spicy dark sauces called moles (pronounced MO-lays). We have tamales. We have burritos and carne asada, thinly sliced beef cooked on the grill. Everything is special.

> *In Merida, Mexico, three girls in traditional dresses hide behind their cotton-candy treats.*

And we eat!

< *As a sign of international cooperation, on April 16, 1998, the United States and Mexico issued almost identical postage stamps celebrating Cinco de Mayo.*

We celebrate our roots.

We celebrate Cinco de Mayo to remember the victory of the Battle of Puebla, so long ago. We celebrate our determination and our willingness to face European forces much stronger than our own.

> *Girls jump rope in front of a huge mural in San Antonio, Texas.*

Every year on Cinco de Mayo we celebrate our heritage, our roots, and our culture. We are proud. And we remember to shout: *¡Viva Mexico!* Long live Mexico!

¡Viva Cinco de Mayo!

In Denver, a boy grins with pride as he flies the Mexican flag over his shoulders.

MORE ABOUT CINCO DE MAYO

Contents

Just the Facts

WHO CELEBRATES IT: It is celebrated mainly in Mexico and the United States.

WHAT: A day to remember the victory of the Battle of Puebla, Mexico, which occurred on May 5, 1862.

WHEN: May 5, but celebrations are sometimes held on the closest weekend.

RITUALS: Parades, dancing, eating Mexican food and celebrating Mexican and Mexican-American customs. Reenacting the battle. Dressing in traditional clothing and decorating with the colors of the Mexican flag.

FOOD: Tortillas, carnes (meats), rice, beans, chiles, sauces. Many families pride themselves on their tamales, which are made from corn flour (masa) and may be filled with anything from sweet corn and raisins to spicy pork, beef, or chicken, then wrapped in corn husks for steaming.

La Raspa: A Mexican Folk Dance

There are many variations on this dance. Here is just one. You can go to http://www.alegria.org/ to learn more about Mexican dance, or folklorico.

Gather in pairs, preferably a boy and a girl in each. Form a circle.

PART 1

Hop on your left foot, and bring your right heel out, touching the ground with toe pointed up and leg straight. Now hop on your right foot, and bring your left heel out, touching the ground with toe pointed up and leg straight. Repeat with left foot. So it's right leg out, then left, then right. Clap two times.

Now do the same thing, but in reverse. Start by hopping on your right foot, bringing your left heel out. So it's left, right, left. Clap two times. Repeat part 1.

PART 2

Each couple links right elbows, one facing front and one facing back, and skips clockwise for a count of 8. Then reverse it: Link left elbows and skip counterclockwise for a count of 8.

Celebrating Cinco de Mayo Around the U.S.

As you can see in the pictures of this book, Cinco de Mayo is celebrated throughout the United States. With a computer, you can easily find out what is happening near you: Search Google, or Ask.com, and type in your town (or a nearby larger town), the word "Cinco," and the year.

Denver boasts one of the biggest parades of lowrider cars, bicycles, and tricycles as they cruise down Federal Boulevard.

Portland, Oregon, features a naturalization ceremony on Cinco de Mayo, in which people are granted United States citizenship. The celebration isn't for Mexicans only.

It includes people from many other countries as well.

There are chihuahua dog races in many places, but Chandler, Arizona, may hold the most famous one. Not only do the little dogs run, Chandler has a "fashion show," and the town crowns a Queen and King Chihuahua.

New York City always has a good show on Cinco de Mayo, as does Port Huron, Wisconsin; Independence, Kansas; and Washington, D.C.

Find out what's going on around you!

ʌ *This lowrider car featured in a parade in Detroit, Michigan, looks like it's dancing.*

My Brother's Burrito Buffet

W hen he was in high school, my younger brother and his friends perfected an easy version of bean and cheese burritos. The toppings would change, depending on what they found in the cupboards or in the refrigerator. As this recipe calls for using the stove, a cutting board, and a knife, you should ask an adult to help.

INGREDIENTS:
Flour tortillas (medium sized)
Refried beans (1 or 2 cans depending on the number of people)
Salsa
Cheese (grated or shredded in packets)

OPTIONAL TOPPINGS:
Canned mild green chilies, diced tomatoes, or sliced black olives (drain the extra liquid). Fresh chopped lettuce, avocado, tomatoes, or onions. Sour cream is always good!

YOU WILL NEED:
Foil, a saucepan, a can opener, a colander, a cutting board and knife, small bowls, and spoons. Plates and napkins for each friend.

1. Preheat the oven to 300 degrees.

2. Count out one tortilla for each person.

3. Wrap the tortillas in foil and put them in the oven for 6–10 minutes.

4. Open the canned refried beans and put them in the saucepan. Stir. Put the pan on a burner and set the heat to medium. When they start to bubble, stir the beans again, then turn the heat to low.

5. Ask your friends to help. Open the salsa. Open and drain the liquid from the canned ingredients. Chop the other ingredients. Put the optional toppings in a bowl with a spoon and put the bowls on the table.

6. When the beans are warm and the toppings are ready, use hot pads to unwrap the foil around the tortillas. Take one tortilla at a time, put it on a plate, and spread 2–3 tablespoons of beans in the middle. Sprinkle lots of grated or shredded cheese on top.

7. Your friends can start topping their own burrito as you make the others.

8. Turn off all the heat and make a burrito for yourself.

9. To fold a burrito, turn one end of the tortilla over the filling, then roll and tuck one side around the middle. One end is open—that's where you start eating!

Find Out More

BOOKS

Those with a star (*) are especially good for children.

Kagan, Neil, editor. *The Concise History of the World*. National Geographic, 2005. This is a large timetable of history; you can see what was going on during and around the Mexican conflict with France.

Kennedy, Diana. *The Essential Cuisines of Mexico*. Clarkson Potter, 2000. A delightful gathering of wonderful recipes.

*Levy, Janice. *Celebrate! It's Cinco de Mayo!* Albert Whitman & Company, 2007. This book is bilingual and fun!

*Menard, Valerie. *The Latino Holiday Book: From Cinco de Mayo to Dia de los Muertos*. Marlowe & Company, 2000.

*Parnwell, E.C., editor, and Sergio Gaitan, translator. *The New Oxford Picture Dictionary*. New Oxford, 1989. Illustrations and arrows help you to learn new words in Spanish— and in English.

Rombauer, Irma S., Becker, Marion Rombauer Becker, and Ethan Becker. *The Joy of Cooking*. Simon & Schuster, Inc., 2006. This kitchen staple has a number of simple recipes for Mexican foods.

WEB SITES

As usual, I consulted Google, Ask Jeeves, and Wikipedia for links. These sites were outstanding:

history.com/history of the holidays
History.com is one of the really important sites on the web.

kiddyhouse.com
For kids, this is what you want to know to sound smart in class!

Mexonline.com
A source of information about all things Mexican.

zianet.com
This site has answers, questions, and puzzles.

Hurrah for the Red, White, and Green!

The flag of Mexico is green, white, and red. In the middle (white) section, there is a picture of an eagle perched on a cactus, holding a snake in its talons. According to legend, when the Aztec were searching for the right place to live, they were supposed to look for the cactus, eagle, and snake. When they found Lake Texcoco, they saw the three living symbols together, and settled in the area now occupied by Mexico City.

Cheering for Mexico at the World Cup in Germany

Glossary

Fiesta: A party or celebration.

Folklorico (fok-LOR-i-co): Means "of the folk" or "of the people." Folklorico dancers perform traditional dances to traditional music.

Lowriders: Specially designed cars or bicycles that may have pneumatic "lifts" (air-filled jacks), so they can jump and bounce and dance.

Maraca (ma-RA-ka): Dried hollow gourds with seeds or pebbles inside, often with a long handle. You shake maracas to the rhythm of the music.

Mariachi (mar-ee-AH-chee): A style of Mexican music that originated in the state of Jalisco. To listen, try MariachiRadio.com.

Naturalization (na-che-ra-le-ZEY-shen): A process in which a citizen of another country is recognized as an American citizen by the U.S. government.

Re-create or reenact: To act out an event; to try to show an audience what took place and how.

Sombrero: A wide-brimmed hat to shelter a person from the sun.

Where This Book's Photos Were Taken

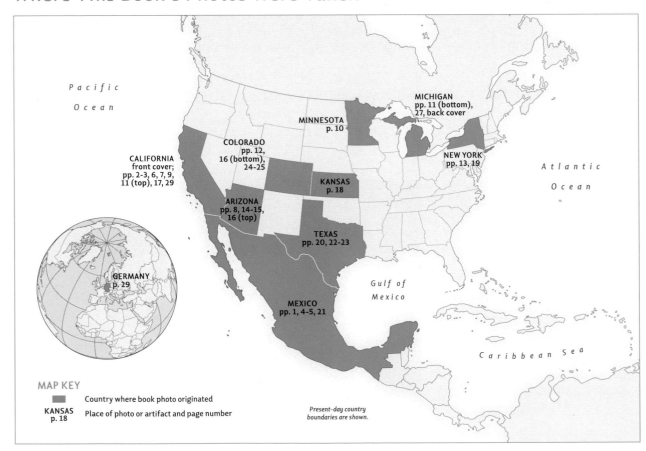

Pacific Ocean

MICHIGAN
pp. 11 (bottom),
27, back cover

MINNESOTA
p. 10

COLORADO
pp. 12,
16 (bottom),
24-25

CALIFORNIA
front cover;
pp. 2-3, 6, 7, 9,
11 (top), 17, 29

NEW YORK
pp. 13, 19

Atlantic Ocean

KANSAS
p. 18

ARIZONA
pp. 8, 14-15,
16 (top)

TEXAS
pp. 20, 22-23

GERMANY
p. 29

Gulf of Mexico

MEXICO
pp. 1, 4-5, 21

Caribbean Sea

MAP KEY

Country where book photo originated

KANSAS
p. 18   Place of photo or artifact and page number

Present-day country boundaries are shown.

30

Cinco de Mayo: A Celebration of Mexican-American Culture

by Dr. José M. Alamillo

To fully understand the historical significance and widespread popularity of Cinco de Mayo in the United States, it is important to view the holiday within the context of Latino history.

After the Mexican victory at the Battle of Puebla on May 5, 1862, President Benito Juárez declared the day a national holiday. Despite the victory, however, the French army returned a year later to defeat the Mexican army and occupy the country. When news of the French occupation reached the United States, the Mexican expatriate community began organizing fundraising events to send money to Mexican troops. By commemorating the Battle of Puebla on May 5th, political exiles and immigrants sought to inspire a resistance movement to oust the French and reclaim Mexico for the Mexicans. After Mexico defeated France and reestablished their independence, these events grew into Cinco de Mayo celebrations that continued into the 20th century.

As more immigrants left Mexico for the United States for economic and political reasons, including a civil war, Cinco de Mayo observances became more patriotic. Besides listening to patriotic speeches, watching parades, and dancing to music, everyone gathered for the coronation of the Cinco de Mayo queen by a Mexican official.

By the 1930s and 1940s, these celebrations had become bilingual and bicultural. Second-generation Mexican Americans, including returning veterans from World War II, associated more with American culture and less with Mexico. Now the celebrations became city wide and included Mexican and American flags, singing of both national anthems, and dancing to American popular music. They became city-wide events. These changes allowed Mexican Americans to build bridges with Anglo Americans and helped residents foster better relations between the two communities.

Inspired by the civil rights movement of the 1960s and 1970s, young Mexican Americans sought to reclaim their history and culture by organizing Cinco de Mayo celebrations in high schools and college campuses. For them, the lesson of self-determination taken from the Battle of Puebla meant that despite overwhelming odds, the Mexican-American community must continue to fight for equal education, political representation, and economic justice. One of these victories was the 1968 Bilingual Education Act, which encouraged public schools to develop bilingual programs and multicultural curriculums.

With increased immigration and the rising buying power of Latino consumers, Cinco de Mayo has continued to change. One reason that the celebrations have become more popular in the United States than in Mexico is that U.S. companies now sponsor, promote, and market the day as a Latino holiday. Corporate America spends millions to reach this growing, youthful, and increasingly middle class market. The geographical dispersion of the Mexican population throughout the country, including unexpected places like the Midwest and South, as well as Hawaii and Alaska, has also contributed to Cinco de Mayo's popularity.

Over the years, Cinco de Mayo has evolved from a minor holiday in Mexico to a popular Latino holiday in the United States. Mexican immigrants celebrate Cinco de Mayo as a way to remember their history, take pride in their culture, raise funds for social causes, and build a sense of community. Today, Cinco de Mayo continues to grow in popularity, becoming a true American holiday.

José M. Alamillo

Dr. José M. Alamillo is an associate professor of Comparative Ethnic Studies at Washington State University. He is the author of Making Lemonade Out of Lemons, *a study of Mexican-American labor and leisure.*

For Roberto, Alberto y Aurora y la familia

PICTURE CREDITS
Front cover, © Kevork Djansezian/ Associated Press; Back Cover: © Ilene MacDonald / Alamy; spine: © Gordon Swanson/ Shutterstock; 1: © Jack Kurtz/ ZUMA Press; 2-3: © Robert Galbraith/ Corbis; 3 (right): © Brand X; 4-5: © Tibor Bogan/ Corbis; 6: © Richard Cummins/ Corbis; 7: © Richard Cummins/ Corbis; 8: © Joe Viesti/ Viesti Associates; 9: © Brian Baer/ Sacramento Bee/ ZUMA Press; 10: © Eric Miller/ Associated Press; 11 (top): © David Young/ Photo Edit Inc; 11 (bottom): © Ilene MacDonald/ Alamy; 12: © Darius Panahpour; 13: © Bryan Smith/ ZUMA Press; 14-15: © Jack Kurtz / The Image Works; 15 top: © Brand X; 16 (top): © Tom Boggan/ Scottsdale Tribune; 16 (bottom): © Darius Panahpour; 17: © Michael Owen Baker / Los Angeles Daily News/ Associated Press; 18: © Karen Lee Milkos / Daily Reporter/ Associated Press; 19 (top): © Brand X; 19 (bottom): © Gary Walts / The Image Works; 20: © Joel Andrews / The Lufkin Daily News/ Associated Press; 21: © Tony Anderson / Getty Images; 22 (left): © USPS/ Associated Press; 22-23: © Philip Gould / Corbis; 24-25: © Darius Panahpour; 27: © Suzanne Tucker/ Shutterstock; 28: © Anthony Hall/ Shutterstock; 29: © Patrik Stollarz/AFP/Getty Images.

Library of Congress Cataloging-in-Publication Data
Otto, Carolyn.
 Celebrate Cinco de Mayo / Carolyn Otto ; Consultant, Jose M. Alamillo.
   p. cm. — (Holidays around the world)
 Includes bibliographical references and index.
 ISBN 978-1-4263-0215-2 (trade : alk. paper) —
 ISBN 978-1-4263-0216-9 (library : alk. paper)
 1. Cinco de Mayo (Mexican holiday) — Juvenile literature. 2. Cinco de Mayo, Battle of, Puebla, Mexico, 1862 — Juvenile literature. I. Alamillo, José M. II. Title.
 F1233.O88 2008
 394.262—dc22

                   2007034250

Series design by 3+Co. and Jim Hiscott.
The body text in the book is set in Mrs. Eaves.
The display text is Lisboa.

Front cover: Dancers from the Alegria Mexicana group perform a traditional Mexican dance during a Cinco de Mayo celebration in Los Angeles, California.
Back cover: Mexican Americans in Port Huron, Michigan, set off for their community's Cinco de Mayo festival.

Title page: Carrying a Mexican flag, a boy hurries to join a parade in Mexico City, Mexico.

Founded in 1888, the National Geographic Society is one of the largest nonprofit scientific and educational organizations in the world. It reaches more than 285 million people worldwide each month through its official journal, NATIONAL GEOGRAPHIC, and its four other magazines; the National Geographic Channel; television documentaries; radio programs; films; books; videos and DVDs; maps; and interactive media. National Geographic has funded more than 8,000 scientific research projects and supports an education program combating geographic illiteracy.

For more information, please call 1-800-NGS LINE (647-5463) or write to the following address:
National Geographic Society
1145 17th Street N.W., Washington, D.C. 20036-4688 U.S.A.

Visit us online at www.nationalgeographic.com/books

For information about special discounts for bulk purchases, please contact National Geographic Books Special Sales: ngspecsales@ngs.org. For rights or permissions inquiries, please contact National Geographic Books Subsidiary Rights: ngbookrights@ngs.org

ACKNOWLEDGMENTS
Saludos y gracias to José Alamillo, the consultant for this book. Huge big *abrazos* (hugs) for Venda and her daughter, Sharon Amann Feld, a bilingual teacher in Phoenix who believes education works both ways, and to her students, who sent descriptions and drawings of their Cinco de Mayo celebrations. And thanks to Mary Beth and Nancy, whose support is integral.